Yokum Reflections

Robert Augustin Regnier

authorHOUSE®

AuthorHouse™
1663 Liberty Drive
Bloomington, IN 47403
www.authorhouse.com
Phone: 1-800-839-8640

Published by AuthorHouse   02/19/2015

ISBN: 978-1-4969-6090-0 (sc)
ISBN: 978-1-4969-6089-4 (e)

Library of Congress Control Number: 2014922592

Print information available on the last page.

Any people depicted in stock imagery provided by Thinkstock are models,
and such images are being used for illustrative purposes only.
Certain stock imagery © Thinkstock.

This book is printed on acid-free paper.

Glow That's Clear

Can I crash here tonight?
I got nowhere to go
I can feel the hunger
And I feel it grow
Inside my body
And through my soul
Please make it go lightly
And make me whole
Nancy loved the flowers
They warmed her heart
A gift given to express our love
The flowers say "We'll never part"
There's a full moon tonight
And it says "love is here"
Light shining down in the night
Brings a glow that's very clear

Time to Build

It's time to build
Put your tool belt on
Get out your hammer and saw
Build a house to gaze upon
A house with spirit
And room for all
Rooms with windows made of glass
And a chimney that stands tall
Nancy did this
And many other things
She helped with a song
A melody that brings
Everybody together
Carpenters, plumbers, painters with paint
This house will take time to build
But yes we can wait

Today You'll find

You can dress a monkey up
But you can't take him to dinner
Put a bow tie around his neck
And make him a winner
But time told me
Paris was the place
To write a book
About a woman dressed in lace
What stories
Do you want to tell
The fairy does the magic
And she does it well
So in Alabama
The peach tree grows
From the ground and to the sky
A victory we all know

We Believe

Go do it
When you sleep and dream
Lightning storm in the sky
On the table is milk and cream
Not beholden to one
Or another sound
Believe in tomorrow
And music in this town
On the mountain
I am the way
See the girl dance
I love this café
So line it up
The band plays a tune
Go pick flowers
In the middle of June

Hummingbird Come Back

The Hummingbird never came back
To the flowers that point in the sky
We hope he's well
But we don't know why
He never came back
To the garden we hold
In deep respect
So let the story be bold
And tell a tale that's real
With a happy happy end
Come back little hummingbird
You are my friend

The Beast and His Friend

We're the only ones in this castle
Aren't we beast
Can I go through the walls
And at least
See the stars
Shine in the sky
Go in a rocket ship
And try
Not to dream
Of her and the song
She sings every night
With a voice always strong
Put your fingers together
And pray you need me
To weather the storm
The clouds and the rain we see

Going Back

The queen of the teens
Told me fear's a choice
Courage when I dream
And find my voice
Presenting a song
Harmony close to the vest
Dreaming my life away
This music is the best
What else can I do
My tears fell like rain
In lonesome town
Where the song killed the pain
So for my darling
With you I belong
Thinking about where
Our love will be strong

Going Deep Going Strong

A red glass
With a red straw
A better picture
You couldn't draw
Is it the drink
A bottle of wine
You got me going
Seeing a warning sign
Piano plays a song
And you and I sing along
High notes, low notes
All of them strong
Can you take me higher
With love from me to you
I'm begging you please
To keep our love true

Sharp Tools

Men know wood
It grows in trees
Cut the boards the sawmill sees
The home of honey bees
Two by fours
And plywood grows
Under the barrel, under the nose
Of the dressmaker that sews
Frame a cabin
With sharp tools
The bubble in the level rules
The ones who think different are never fools
Throw shade
And pails of sand
On the beach, across the land
Where eyes see a vision that's grand

Sugarcane Sweet

Sugarcane sweet
Where our eyes meet
And see the sky blue
In a wideness that's true
So let me hold on
And gaze upon
The flower that grows
Up before the ground froze
Under our feet
And in the seat
Of the pilot of spin
That worships within
The mind of a ghost
And the darkness of most
Champions that see
Brightness for you and me

Many Many Goods

It's coming
The coming
Of fear of the dance
And emotional drumming
Teach me some moves
Draw me a line
Go to the post
Of the welcoming sign
The roof reaches up
And points to the sky
Where airplanes and eagles
Fly side by side and try
To be the best
Never playing games in the sand
A new landscape
A new creation on the land

When You and I Meet

Look look
Down down
Over the fence
And all around
The field that is green
Growing crops of wheat
To supply a feast
Where you and I could meet
And see the sun
Cross the sky
A sky of blue
Where clouds go bye
So write a book
With words that say
Time has come
For you and me today

The Sails We Set

Speed is our captain
Lightning in the night
The song of the wind chime
Sings with birds in flight
Can it be
Crying eyes of gold
Look at the young girl
Coming in from the cold
Her skin was soft
Like supple emotional leather
She dances with silver toes
Where the song will let her
Have a grand view
Of the wind that's blowing
In the sails we set
And the candles that are glowing

Heart And Soul

Yes my heart will deceive
And it's only make believe
Promise that it isn't so
That I'll never let you go
Cry your troubles away
With rain on a sunny day
Time came for me to come
Over to the park where we could get some
Berries and apples and tomatoes in a can
Fruit for a feast for our fellow man
Straight and strong and kind
Love is only on my mind
So put some coal in the stove
Large and flashy was the car I drove
But the song my ears will hear
Will always be dear

Lions Roar

Give me the hammer
Power and nails
The ships of love
Tell no tales
I don't mind seeing
A cool man down
Playing his guitar
On a stage in swing town
I've been told
Good days are coming
Around the corner, around the bend
With care and lots of loving
So run and run
And run some more
The race to raining rock
Will end with a lion's roar

The Road We Take

Two lanes of freedom
For you and me brother
You take one
I'll take the other
One goes south
One goes west
I'm not saying anything
Both are the best
But don't you know
That kisses are sweet
At the end of the road
Where the sun and the sky meet
So we're both running
Against the wind and to a star
Sing a little song
And keep on trucking, we will go far

My Feelings For You

When you're feeling lonely
When you're hiding in your bed
When flowers will not grow
And your feelings for me are dead
I will still pick apples
For you and find
The words to a song
That show you I'm a kind
Writer of poems
And a sweet hearted man
A cradle of caring
Doing the best that I can
So listen
To the wind blowing through a tree
And feel a new life
Coming alive for you and me

A Train Headed South

I took a train headed south
Didn't know where I was going
My mind was ready for anything
Going where the wind was blowing
Fly, fly away
Like a bird from it's nest
Traveling to a place in the sun
Yes I think it's for the best
She broke my heart
Because our love wasn't true
I'm a lonely child
With feelings sad and blue
But I think things will be better
When I get to the mouth
Of the river flowing gently
By the train headed south

A Voice In The Moment

It started with the voice
Saying words, a speaking tongue
Take a trip down the river
Look around, the song is sung
This is the moment
You got to see what I see
A blue bird in the sky
A squirrel in a tree
We're sorry you've lost
Your mate and a good friend
We've seen many changes
Changes that lend
Us to a song
We sing every day
To while away the mornings
In sunshine, a spiritual way

19

Celtic Twilight

You got to see
What I see
I see the floor rumble
And shake like a tree
Infected with fever
And a cold sweat
But when we rock steady
Time will let
Us see the stars
And the light that shines
Up from the heart
And a road of straight lines
So the poets of the past
Go quietly in the night
With the emotion of the words
Of Celtic twilight

Standing Water

Walking in the rain
Looking lost
The movement is growing
But at what cost
One in a hundred
The last man standing
In front of the fire pit
Where the flames are never ending
Tread lightly
And seize the doll
Left on the door step
A gift for all
So temporary or long term
Love will come to be
In the form of a cross
Cut from an oak tree

That Song

That song

I thought I knew

Was sung

By the girl with the rose tat-too

Lost in a zone

But found on a wave

On an uncharted map

Of the home of the brave

I thought I'd be alone forever

Searching through pictures of the past

Images of days gone bye

Are memories that will last

So take me to the other side

Of the garden of open desire

Yes my body was singed

By flames of hell's fire

Its About The Night

We talked into the night
About the soul of a tree
Sand dunes by the sea
Ambitious art for you and me
Take a walk
Up a hill
To see the irises and the daffodil
Grow high above the morning chill
Vincent gave us many things
He loved the country side
Where he took a donkey ride
And his brushes never lied
So I'm a grandfather
And I search for a song
With a voice that's strong
Down a road that's long

Join Us

Dear Nancy
Did you know I'm blue
That my eyes are blue
That the sky is the color blue
Got to be lucky
To say
That making love is the way
To read words that say
That you and I are strong
And wise in our thinking
About forces that are linking
Us to cold water we are drinking
So let the legends fight
A battle that can't be won
By the sword and by the gun
By kings blessed by the sun

Ramblings On A Summer Day

Wrong a right
It's a bad thing in the night
You'll never be lonely no more
Because pleasure is what we have in store
Frozen thoughts in the household
It's the fun part that's bold
When I finished writing it
We sang the song and it was time to quit
Who doesn't love a good fight
Punches will fly into the night
Keep everyone calm
The soldiers will find the bomb
She hasn't aged in years
But going it alone is one of her fears
So stay in the park, because the band will play
Songs of the night, played on this sunny day

Angels Never Cry

Looking forward
By looking back
Cosmic eyes
Are what we lack
But we see the vision
Of days gone bye
In the fruits of our labor
And the tears we cry
Take a long look
At shadows in the night
They shine in the dark
Of moon and starlight
So take me to the sun
The bright star in the sky
Where darkness is never seen
And where angels never cry

Night Garden

My garden lives at night
Quiet in the day
Tip – toe around the hot rocks
Growing life is the way
The further back in time I travel
With friends into the night
Not for a season or even a century
Will I scurry with birds in flight
The sunlight goes down
And yes it's great
To see the sunset, ever so pretty
Nocturnal dinner served on a silver plate
So I work in my garden
Only at night
Moon and star light makes it grow
For everyone's delight

Follow Me To Paradise

I wanted love

I needed love

To see me through

To a place from above

And a new beginning

Where happiness rides

On the wings of an eagle

That fishes in the skies

Tonight we will sing

And take a long look

At the happy life

Seen in the pages of the young girl's book

So whoever cries

Tears of joy and pleasure

Will dance behind the apple tree

The breath of a natural treasure

Pull Us All Together

The forecast calls for thunder
Lightening and rain
Stormy weather
That reaches past the pain
Time makes two
Of us and a broken heart
And because of me
Words of love will never part
Reach down deep
Into your pockets for gold
Blues guitar needs strings
Hear them play songs from the cold
Time tied to a bottle
Thrown in the ocean with dreams
In our minds and our hearts
The journey we take is not what it seems

The Bear Sets The Mark

When I eat strawberries
My lips turn blue
But they're already there
Yes it's true
All these people
Walk a straight line
Suggestions given freely
So give me a sign
Thunder and lighting
A picture of Tweety Bird
Unburden yourself, but at what cost
Sweep us away with a timeless word
So find pleasure from the top
With a name that's very dark
Go see the sun
The bear sets the mark

The Farmers Field

Fish in a small brook
Catch a few
The cow goes moo
Start at sunrise, yes we do
Drive the horse in the field
And we cut the hay
Catch our berries in pots of clay
On the farm we stay
Put money in your pocket
And take a journey home
Stay in place the hair we comb
Square dance under the dome
So create the future
Unlock the truth
The painter is long in the tooth
Superman in a telephone booth

What Did You See

Show us a candle

Light up the night

What did you see

Was it a ghost, spirit in sight

The author spoke a name

His lips said a lot

The girl and her dress

That time forgot

The black nurse

Stays in sync

With the drama that unfolds

But what will she think

When five adds up to one

And the answers are hard to come bye

The camera shows the pictures

And winning the game is something we try

We All Stand Tall

Boom
And we're surprised
That true freedom
Tell no lies
It's nice and bright
The sun is high
A breeze is blowing
No clouds in the sky
Nancy and I pray
For peace and common love
This land is our land
Sent to us from above
So there it goes
Our love for all
Take it quietly into the night
Where we all stand tall

Aquarius

I felt flushed with fever
My body had a cold sweat
But time gave me you and a song
On the merry-go-round where we met
The girl who wrote the song
Told me I got what it takes
Come in whip, the door opens
To a poem dedicated to love that makes
You happy in the course
Of the river flowing past
No matter where you are
Because the love we have will last
Into the night
And into the day
So keep on trying
Because love will find a way

Through Out The Night

Never believe
That it's not so
Even in the valley
Where the flowers grow
You're close to me
Even when you're away
Letters are sent
And memories stay
Close to the top
Of the bottom that's down
So come to me
And we'll play music in our town
Prepare yourself
And it will come out right
All together as one
Together throughout the night

Then Came You

Gotta turn it up loud

My DJ told me

Tell me more, tell me more

And my eyes will see

Love in the back seat of a car

Where hugs and kisses flow free

And fireworks fly

Where we

Find mysteries without clues

Far away and in

The valley of the dolls

Where love will always win

So nothing is true

Many things are a lie

But I have you

And I never have to say goodbye

The Evening Star

Her hands are never cold
Her eyes are always bright and clear
She starts her day with a song
Another morning with music keep near
A summer breeze
Gliding through the arms
Of young girls dancing
And showing the world their young girl charms
Take a flower
Just one will do
Place it in her hand
It means so much for me and you
That a stroll in the woods
Will take us far
Into the night
When twilight will gives us the evening star

At The Beginning

At the beginning of another night
I will hold you ever tight
On the ring of an open fire
It will burn with strong desire
So thank you for this morning kiss
Given sweetly in a place like this
The song of the mountain
Is sung by the man of tin
Your daddy is rich
And an open door sees a witch
We dance up and down
In the streets of swing town
This chain is strong
When we pull the weight, we can't go wrong
So when we put it out there, on the line
Not a dry eye will we find

Thorns On Green Stems

They told me
Granma wore this
Around her neck with pride
A stone set in gold, sealed with a kiss
A hand shake was given
In a sea of red tracers
Saddle up boys, the road is long
We're just one of the racers
I stepped clear
Of any danger that we saw
He said we needed water
At the well where we draw
So he stood by himself
Alone in the garden of white
Roses with thorns on green stems
He cast his shadow in the night

Find Forever

Don't say a word
Your body says it all
Soft as satin but strong as steel
Find pleasure under a waterfall
I wish I had time
To read the book of rhymes
Or messages from the little ones
But we hear music from the wind chimes
I want an easy touch
A slow hand with a calm head
This story will be for everyone
When everything is said
The horse and the wagon gear up
To travel down the road
But when they cross the bridge
They find forever and this story is told

When I Danced

I'm not a dancer anymore
But who am I
Maybe a singer of songs
But I sometimes cry
Tears that run down my face
That stain the soul inside
A body that has seen greatness
And took a wonderful ride
On a stage with lights
That shined up and down
On me when I danced
With grace in this town

The Road We Travel

They asked me how I felt
But what could I say
That I was blue and feeling down
Sad and lonely on this rainy day
But when I saw birds
Fly in flocks in the sky
I felt better all around
But I did wonder why
The song I heard in the wind
Was a tune that flowed free
Down the valley and trough the trees
A melody that lovers would see
In their lives
And in their dreams
But the road we travel
Is not what it seems

Going Where The Weather Suits My Clothes

I don't even know how
To hold your hand
Or draw circles in the sand
Ride horses across the land
Take me baby
And give me love
Because I'm thinking of
You and me and spirits from above
But will you love me tomorrow
And many days after
Days that are filled with laughter
The song is old, oh what does it matter
But I can tell
That in your eye there is a tear
Sweet and soft, there is no fear
And in the woods lives the deer

Forever Is Where we Are

Look out kid
You're going to get hit
With a pie in the face
Squarely in the chair where you sit
Send me a bottle
Of night train wine
Hail, hail the wrecking ball
Breaking down the welcoming sign
The daily rhythm of life
Let the games begin
The trees are for lovers
When we laugh, we all win
So play old songs
With the base, the fiddle, and the guitar
Oh my darling the work is hard
Because forever is where we are

Feeling Ok

I don't know where
But she takes me there
To a place that has sunny skies
A place we enjoy without a care
No matter how you toss the dice
It will come to an end soon
To see what America was like
"Sugar pie, honey bunch" was the tune
So send it along
With love because it hurt so bad
In the heart and in the soul
Where her eyes looked so sad
The vines are made for baskets
Bees were made for honey
How should you do it, tell the truth
Just find the words that sound funny

Folk Music Song

I want to sleep in your clover
Dream in green fields
Stop the war, sing for freedom
The knights hide behind their shields
It's a delight to hear it
A song where fairy tales come true
Take me to that wonder place
Where guitars play for me and you
So shout out the words
And find stars we can reach
The music of her laughter comes
When the time is here, we will teach
Together we will get there
But when I don't know
Consider being part of the promised land
Where a jingle jangle feeling will grow

The only Life We Know

Hey hey, it's me
Just singing a song, letting it be
Violet is the color, ever bright
A flower that shines in the night
Rocking and a rolling, punches fly
But why do they fight, we wonder why
I can't live with out her, or in
The stage of a cabaret or the games we win
Getting ready to take the stage
Reckless and beautiful, it's all the rage
Bad timing will ruin it all
For all the dancers at the curtain call
Under the light, behind the tree
Will we be angry, I guess we'll see
But you look so fine, in your blue dress
Your style and grace is heads above the rest

The Lucky One

Her face changed from terrified to dull
Her appetite went away
Lines formed on her for head and hands
Sadly this was just another day
She said "Take me away"
"I can't take it anymore"
Her mind went slowly
Though the open door
And the wind saw it all
Perfect colors of red and blue
The painter was on the other side
With writers of fairy tales, searching without a clue
So they all danced
With trepid feet around the sign post
But who will be the lucky one
The one who is strong, or the one with the most

Holding On

Holding on to
A revolution that has a wheel
And a spoke and the feel
Of black metal, iron and steel
Holding on to
Clouds that fill a sky of blue
With no time left for me and you
For our love is true
Holding on to
A picture of you and a song
A book of words that are strong
Memories that will travel a road that's long
So I'm barely holding on to
A picture, a memory that will tell
Of sounds and ripples in the wishing well
The gap in the forest where the tree fell

Pink

What is the opposite of pink?

It's not a primary color

Or a soft shade

Of sweet caramel butter

Maybe the feel

Of a warm summer night

The bristles of cactus

Or the glow of moon light

It is a puzzle

But I will find the answer

To this terrible dilemma

That is this mind bender

A Simple Act Of God

A simple act of God
In a storm
Brought us together
And made our hearts feel warm
But can I connect to it
Can I sing
A song that will brings us hope
In these late days of spring
This is country music
Nobody can make it any better
I walk alone
On a road to better weather
So listen boy
Tell her about the different way
That you and I feel
About love, beauty and a natural day

I Would Rather Watch
the Flowers Grow

She's up there now
But will she be alright
Will laughter fill the night
When will the wind fly the kite
I thought she was immortal
But her soul danced with grace
In the halls of a sacred place
Where evil left her without a trace
Someday
We will come back for more
And eat an apple to the core
Good news, bad news, what do we have in store
But I'm afraid I can't help you
Sorry but I have to go
I'm cursed to going slow
I'd rather watch the flowers grow

The Way We Are

Tell me why we're here
Maybe because the grass is green
Players like us just like to be seen
An open mind is always clean
What will we come too
Holding on to your lovers hand
Playing ball on a beach of sand
Riding horses across the land
But what will we see?
A statue with arms of gold
Ice cream cones that are cold
The happy ending of a story told
So stay the way you are
Because condors fly high
And glide forever in the sky
A feat we would love to try

So Lets Just Beat It

Good looking woman
Sleeps in deep thought
And dreams of flying saucers
Where weird science is bought
Excitement time
Beats the heat
Secrets and surprises
At the end of an lonely street
We were talking a minute ago
When Nancy took a look
At pictures of dragon flies
On the pages of an open book
So we refuse to walk alone
With faces that see around
A circle of bright stars
That shines on this mountain town

Sweetly On A Sunny Day

I'll never lose that feeling
Of funky music leading the way
To quieter Times
That say
Let my love open the door
To funky street
On the other side of town
Where hep cats like us meet
So it all comes down
To us finding the way
To sing our songs
Sweetly on a sunny day

Art Is Never Finished

The days we were alone
Were like scratches on a stone
We had to find another song
Because the words and melody were wrong
Maybe a book, or maybe not
A walk in the park is what we want
A cup of coffee in the morn
A new day is born
Put this on your shoulder, it's cold
The pain was rough, the story was told
The price we pay for saying good bye
Will shape our lives and make us cry
So chances are very good
That true love will survive as it should

Sixty Four Times Zero

Stay close to the music
Because I can get bye
With the change in my voice
Strong, but not my choice
Front porch sitter will never cry
Go walk in wooden shoes
Tortured, but more is there
In the house of blue
The only home for me and you
She has a silver veil in her hair
A quiet day by the sea
A soulful dance in the park
Let's kiss then light the fire
Sing and find desire
Look down for the errant spark

Running Against the Wind

I feel like yesterday
Was nothing more than a dream
The space in a song
Or the glow of a sunbeam
I had a conversation
In the company of a quiet story
All kinds of apple and oranges
Were in the mix, but not to worry
Because future days are bright
And our ears are tuned in
To the games we play
And the games we win
But I think that good news
Will build a foundation
Of words in a book
An example of our creation

The Countess

Take a deep breath
It's nice to hear music again
And we must not prefer
To be over protective when
Mothers step back
And reach for the moon
Cry themselves to sleep
Grow bright and see very soon
The colors of simple words
That understates the shade
Of summertime blue
In a book where dreams are made
The paper printed her letter
The radio followed along
"Tell the world I'm lonely"
Said the Countess in a song

The Ladder

Take a better picture
Of the imaginary man
Who climbs the ladder
As high as he can
To watch the birds
Fly in the sky
Higher and higher
But will he try
To save his heart
For the one who sees
Passion and song
In the boughs of apple trees
So go to the end
Of a road that's long
To satisfy the whims
Of the warrior who is strong

An Early Book

The freedom to run in a field
The joy that nature brings
Go to work in a theater
It's a family where everybody sings
Give me some sugar
And all things sweet
Find a green field
Where we are sure to meet
Dreams that give silence
To dreamers that open a door
And pray that flowers will grow
From the bottom of the garden floor
So us pilgrims need help
To find a way that sings
Songs that make sense
Of flowers and other things

It Feels Good

It feels good to be home
Again, and in your arms
Where love is a rainbow
And sincere is in your charms
Rise and mix
Our feelings strong
The island is changing
In words and in a song
But what brings me to you
Wasn't heaven or a bolt of light
Just respect for the deep
And eyes of star light bright
Like filming a ballet
In colors all around
Let the dance begin
Let the steps follow the sound

One Memory at a Time

One memory at a time
Paper roses cost a dime
Shoulder a song
Down a road that's long
Feeling out of place
With clothes of satin and lace
But don't drink whiskey on the rocks
Just keep it straight and narrow
Behind keys and locks

We Are All Friends

It isn't going to rain
The scare crow said
In front of the waking dead
Sleeping in their cold hard bed
My God is a mountain mover
Moving rocks and stone
Perched from his high throne
Taking breaths, never alone
Love cuts like a knife
But it feels so right
When celebrated at night
Under moon and starlight
And together we made love
Under the stars that shined above
In spirit with the turtle dove

Courage in Time

It started with
Courage in time
Love in our prime
And a spirit in rhyme
I took a walk down
To a big country place
Where greyhounds race
For prizes of satin and lace
But someday I will
Try not to stray
From staying away
And enjoying this beautiful day

The Strongest Fighter

The strongest fighter
Lives another day
His elegant mate
Is here to stay
The victor finds a place
To swim in the sun
And gather each year
To fight the battle won
As the story goes
The weak challenge the strong
And stay in the picture
Until the bird sings a song
Find the right words
To wiggle and sweep
The darkness of the calm
And the music of the ocean deep

There Are Rules

I'm never going to dance again
Play or write a song
My mind is in a tiff
Because the world has done me wrong
I was in town
When the bird left the place
He flew into the sky
Not leaving a trace
But I enjoy peace of mind
When I step outside
The fence that holds me back
Without a voice or an eye opened wide
My feelings were sealed and hidden
Behind a closed door
But anything a man could wish for
Is his for evermore

Fortune Cookie

A thrilling time
Is in your future
You will have a party
A time that will be finer
You are a person
Of a strong sense of duty
Get your mind set
Away from being moody
Confidence will lead you on
You are a happy man
Your emotional nature
Will help you when it can
Strong and sensitive
You were born
With a silver spoon in your mouth
Teeth of gold
Your future is headed south

Lemon Pie

Let's eat lemon pie
Together on this special night
China plate with a knife and spoon
We enjoy this treat of lovers delight
We work all day
To pay for things
That makes life good
And sometimes brings
A song to sing
On a sunny day
Where the two of us while
Our time away

Barefoot in the Garden

Barefoot in the garden
Where flowers grow tall
Never in a hurry
Just splashing in a waterfall
Chipmunks take notice
Hummingbirds are your friend
Taking care of nature's gift
Together to the end
Colorful peddles
Of red and green
Live under the sun
Just trying to be seen
To lovers holding hands
And strolling in the sun
Beautiful flower garden
Gives hope for it is the one

Its Not Hard To Do

I took the early train
To Swing Town
Dancing all the way
Digging the sound
Ask me about the jewelry
She wore on her head
Diamonds from her ears
Many words were said
That told about going away
To a garden all alone
With a spiritual shrine
Made of wood and stone
So take me to your leader
He swings from a tree
Singing a love song
Just trying to be free

I Must Be Writing

Seasons change
My thoughts get rearranged
I must be lonely
Delighted to share
And be aware
I must be quiet
Why dwell at that now
Stand tall and take a bow
I must be proud
Live with you so I can teach
You, with my feelings in reach
I must be cautious
But then, God blessed the child
His will, and a season mild
I must be happy
A search for a question
An answer with no action
I must be blue
So I write a song
For you and we sing along
I must be a best friend

Fire On the Mountain

One less spark
One less fire
Escape to reality
A little more desire
See the marquee
Display the compass rose
Wood and cloth, iron and steel
Ware a change of woven clothes
Last chance to see a masterpiece
And the glamour of the ride
What is he reading, space in time
Golden hour on the wild side

Always in Control

I didn't mean to turn you on
But I did
Always in control
But I sometimes get rid
Of feelings of grandeur
And an opulent style
Lost in forgiveness
We danced in the spotlight for awhile
Culture club brakes ties
And sings in jest
Their stylish wardrobe
Is the best in the west
So take a bow
We won the battle for today
Fighting for the freedom bell
Are the words we say

Comfortable in our Dreams

It's over and done
But danger is still in front of you
The man in the brimmed hat
Wore leather gloves and chains too
I don't like to see it
A deer killed by a mountain lion
It's hard to talk about and see
Eyes with tears that are crying
Look at that face
It can smell time
Spin inside a magnet
Horizontal strips on a vertical climb
So send signals
And pay attention to what it means
The windows open early
And we are comfortable in our dreams

Winter Rainbow Hat

Winter rainbow hat
On the horn players child
Ride a horse drawn sleigh
On a day that is mild
She likes to sleep on her side
Close to the stripped pillow
But far from the edge
Of the leaves of a weeping willow
Doors close
To a dress colored blue
And shoes that count to five
Odd steps for me and you

Mister Man

Say you're sorry
Mister man
Tell the world
When you can
That ninety nine verses
Carry the day
To racers of glory
With feet of clay
She wore a stripped shirt
Over a body forlorn
That rose up gallantly
But sadly was torn
Between a road of courage
And a path of despair
No holding back
A breath of fresh air

I Feel Power

I feel power from your words
And everything with this sound
Hour by hour, time in the sky
We tell our story in this town
Patching together
A world of survival
Fighting for the love we need
At the time of arrival
It's an exciting big day
When I take my time
On the path I take
And the mountains I climb
So presented with a problem
We think about the stages
That our minds will see
Clearly when we turn the pages

The Show Goes On

The writer of songs
Seemed locked up in chains
Fireworks and streamers
Here come the rains
But where are you Emmy Lou
You're needed here
To save them from themselves
The fan will never shed a tear
So crawl before you walk
Sing before you paint
Emmy Lou Harris
Lives the life of a saint
So they do their show
And the fans like what they see
Cowboy hats and tight fitting jeans
The road beckons for you and me

Special Tribute

I will be a country writer
Behind the scenes, behind the stage
There's no way of knowing
If my sound will be all the rage
But meanwhile I drive your truck
Music and stars
Whisper to me softly
And try to stay out of the bars
Pop, pop, pop
You make me feel whole
You are golden
When the night is as black as coal
I gave the juke box my last dime
So I could hear the song I wrote
That look in your eyes comes alive
Enjoy this song to the last note

A Raspberry Vine

I saw a raspberry vine
Rising from the sea
A fruit of various taste
A vine like a young tree
But the evidence showed
Me being me
Neighbors and goats
Are friends we see
So go to the tournament
And shoot the lights out
Play games to win
So we can sing and shout
The language of the heart
The melody of the soul
The two of us will never part
It feels good to be in control

Benjamin Bauck

Have mercy on her
Benjamin Bauck
Silver knife in a box
Under key and lock
A book we read
Never taking pause
A woman under hat
Begs for coins just because
Come in my lad
The sailor knows the ways
Mark me, the virgin feels the pain
On dark and stormy days

The News

I sell newspapers
On the street
Interesting people
That I meet
Say things that bare fruit
On whimsical ways
Sharing stories
On sunny days
There are many tales
The newspaper tells
Photographers and reporters
Whistles and bells
They all come together
In an effort as one
Sharing the news
For pleasure and fun

Two Hundred Years

I got the one
The monster of widow hill
Just what the truth is
A breeze and a winter chill
Her name was Veronica
Her red hair says it all
Grab me some bolt cutters
And open the gate to the castle wall
Play, the month is cold
Sculptured with tropical ice
Sitting on a treasure trove
Always ready to pay the price
Cursed in this body, for two hundred years
Locked in a box, paddle lock and chain
It's the last war, who will win
Ride to the play on the love train

Aztec Eyes

Dark shadow falls
On Aztec eyes
The wood pile stacks up neatly
And our friend sees only windy skies
Ride to the highest hill
Dismount, and let the horse run free
Freedom lives on top
Vistas clear is everywhere we see
So this is the land of the brave
And the soil of the strong
Flowers grow bright
Nature lives in a song

Time is Running

Nothing on this earth
Will make me turn back
Not the hassles in the way
Or the power that we lack
Walking by myself
On a path by the sea
I stop to sit on a bench
Under a shade tree
So throw me a kiss
And drive us away
To a cottage in the hills
So we can enjoy this holiday

A Man and His Scythe

He was alone in the field
Just him and his scythe
The hay was tall
And no rain in the sky
His work was ahead of him
Sun up to sun down
Hay for the animals
Living close to the ground
So back and forth
His stroke on time
Laboring to the end of the day
When he will hear the dinner bell chime

Heart of Stone

A woman but wise
In reason we see
Legs that carry her away
Bedroom farce can only be
Sunday came
And I dreamt of gentle ways
The humming bird flew back and forth
And hovered in one place
Sardines are packed
As sardines go
Finding room is hard
Does anyone Know?
But her eyes were still
Sitting there alone
Seeing only bright stars
Smiling at a heart of stone

The Work of a Higher Power

I saw the look of love
On the road to big sky
And when I got there
I walked a mile never asking why
She said I'm just like you
And my feelings are clear
It's not what you say
It's what they hear
We talked about the nitty gritty
The name of the dress, life, and law
False views and polarization
Living are the things we saw
So people with big glasses stir the pot
With a spoon made of wood
When explaining what the center would be
I wrote a letter and yes it was good

Tea with You

It's nice having
Tea with you
On chairs and a table
Under a sky of blue
They say we're cute
Holding hands together
Sharing our love
Through sunny and stormy weather
So love is in front of us
Never getting in the way
Always trying hard
Good times are here to stay

The Man of Desert Air

This doorstep has a visitor
From a land very far away
He took his saddle off his horse and walked
Through the church door and started to pray
He lit a candle at the alter rail
Solemn, but he didn't stay long
Off to his hotel room he went
Trying to hide his feelings strong
Morning came early and bright
And it was time for him to leave
He collected his thoughts as best he could
For in God the highest he did believe
Riding away he touched the ones
Who saw him say his prayer
So through that door went a mysterious man
A man who felt the desert air

An Emotion we Felt

There is no darkness on the sun
So come to a place of reason
I can see clearly
Brightness is a change of season
If you're fearless
All things will fall in place
Learn to step back
And you will win the long race
Join me
And view the land
Through glass colored with love
Light through waves of shifting sand
So the blue shadow will fall
Down when I see you dress
And the diamonds you ware
No more time or angels to bless

Your Tomorrow

Take me to your tomorrow
A beam of light in the sky
Call it what you want
A cloud of hope that never asks why
Follow the light to today
A circle brings us around
Make it bright and make it stay
Pleasant is the sound
So speak up my dear
And hide behind a shade tree
Find your voice in song
Melodies that set us free

Rock N Roll Heart

I waited for you
Before there was sunshine
I waited for you
Before days of roses and wine
And the wait was long
Star crossed and trying
Rolling thunder in a music day
The weeping willow never stopped crying
But I think I'll stay here
Because the guitar player sounds so good
I'm enjoying many days
Of flying kites and splitting wood
So make it easy
Simple words in a world complete
With songs and poems that show the way
To a place where treasure and melody meet

Joy from Above

She was in front of a broken mirror
Combing her hair
Skin deep were her feelings
But her love was there to share
Blues singer with an edge
Plays his guitar and sings
A hard rocking song
Up and down goes the wild things
So I introduce you
To song and everlasting love
We sing it with our hearts and soul
And joy from above

Something Special
is Happening

Out the front door
And pushed against the wall
Our love is back home
Good times for one and all
Beautiful and new are the green fields
We try to remember
But now they're covered with snow
In these days of December
Quiet stars in quiet nights
Wonderful sounds show the way
Something special happens
In dreams made of clay
So I found the answer
It was here all the time
In the songs we sing
And the mountains we climb

Loving Ways Meet

Bring it on home Nancy Nancy
In a tree turtle dove
Is a song played on a wooden boat
In the warm grip of true love
With hands and hearts
And a needle so fine
I will sew our love together
With songs and melody that are very kind
So hundred of photos
Tell our story complete
In a place where nature lives
A place where loving ways meet

The Hand I Hold

She's the hand I hold
Walking down a side street
In our home town
Where lovers like us meet
Did you see this tear rolling down
A face of colors that would destroy
A lesser man – But this one
Is filled with confidence and joy
We jumped in
To a pond where fish have their way
But of course they do, in this water of blue
We all enjoy this sunny day

Voices in the Story

Melodies so thick
You have to brush them away
Under tons of dust
That cover up the words we say
The golden circle shouts
Let it all go down
The stranger we saw
Was a painter passing underground
Yes we can hear it
The blue Jay's call in the morning dew
Lady step back
So I can dance once again with you

They Took a Ride

Seth courted Sarah
With his carriage shining bright
Pulled by his handsome horse
The two sallied into the night
They looked at each other
With warm gentle eyes
Eyes that showed a longing way
Eyes that shined in nighttime skies
So Seth and Sarah drove
Around the country side
They stopped to share a kiss
In front of the river wide
So will they get married?
They seemed to be headed that way
Down the primrose path
To their happy wedding day

Black Pete

Everybody cried
When Black Pete got sick
Taking and giving
Thin or thick
Black Pete grew up
In a dark coal mine
Hard work and sacrifice
But love was hard to find
Traveling north
To a shack on a pond
Working where he could
His word was his bond
I remember Black Pete
Bent over, grey, and old
Black Pete was my friend
Let the story be told

Songs of Sunday Night

Stare at me like a painting
Let your eyes see the light
Quietly we could never fit in
With songs of Sunday night
A line was drawn
In the hot blistering sand
It might be hard to discover
The waking breath that lives in this land
So go to the radio
And dial up memories from long ago
Patience is the catchword
That brought us along the way, High and low

A Handsome Barn

A handsome barn sits on a hill
With a cupola so nice
The color is brown, dark is the shade
A home for chipmunks and mice
Space for horses
And the hay they eat
Space for ducks
And their web feet
Farmers built this barn
With hands that saw hard times
They made this barn rise
From dirt where it climbs
So they built peace and good
And brotherhood
A farmer's paradise
That rose out of stone and wood

Inside is Out

Images
They are strong
Trinkets
Subject of a song
We gas up on
Flames of the heart
Live with cultural treasures
Medicine men never part
Our hero's last words
Were carved in stone
Moment of discovery
Hearts never alone
So get some fresh air
Come inside
Inside is out
Oh what a ride

How Sweet It Is

I'm afraid of scared people
Frightened by the lies they tell
But a new day is coming
Crystal blue where all is well
But now
There's a ball of fire in the sky
Watching over us
And never telling a lie
So now I'm digging the snow, the rain
And the bright sunshine
No storm with winds that blow
Will hold back the love that is mine
So your eyes have told me
How much you care
Never can say goodbye
To you, our love, or a future ever fair

Naked Flash

With darkness on the street
Light has a hard way
Of finding a way to say
That the powers to be have feet of clay
We have seen it all before
Children of open desire
Tall tales around the camp fire
The turning away of a brazen liar
If I thought you would have
Taken a long walk in the night
Lifted our spirits ever so bright
I would have kept a good song in sight
So life has become a sweet sounding guitar
Playing and strumming a song
In a world of beauty where we long
For you and I and everybody else to be strong

Stars and Heaven

I saw stars in the west
Above the clouds, the trees
And all the rest
On one star there was a flame
Climbing high into the sky
Primeval was the game
The sky is filled with pins of light
Many worlds can't count them all
Civilizations rise and fall
Brings life to the darkest night
But how many stars will harbor life
I don't know but heaven will show
A connection too, for me and you
Real in the afterlife

We Lost Jacoby

He was rocking back and forth
Thinking of the tallest tree
The eagle that flies above it
To see the top where we sit
No greater sight is there to see
Sam was a tree cutting man
His ax was sharp and bright
Trees would fall
Amid the coyotes call
But they told him to keep nature in sight
Children who love
Images bright
Play in the back yard
With love as a wild card
The little girl dances in the limelight

Winning Smile

The sky and the sea
Say things that have to be
Clipper ships, electric ride
Three dimensional tree
Fight for the game
Dance for days
It's time for the mirror world
Fabulous colorful ways
Many candles
Flaming bright
Westward flights
Fly into the night
So light up the day
With your glamorous smile
Go to the edge of time
And find serenity and the winning style

Colorful Shades

I look in your mystery eyes
And see flowers in a flower cart
Precious lemons, very tart
Loving ways in your heart
Mountain tops where condors fly
Close to the edge of the sky
Natives on the land will always try
So close your eyes and walk on bye
Chic is the color of red and gold
Green and blue and others too
Painters with vision are far and few
Brushes tell tales, let the canvas be true
Splash of color
A light and sunny shade
Sunshine on the porch, watch it fade
Colorful threads in the clothes we made

The Raven Flies

The raven perches on the window sill
His shadow lays against the door
Dark spirits he brings
Threatening skies and wild things
Eyes that are sharp watch the raven soar
He goes up, high toward the clouds
Flying high he kisses the sun
The raven does his flying alone
Other birds fall back like a stone
Dark is the night for he is the one
Swirling trays of black dust
Are a symbol of who we are
So turn on the water
Make it cold then hotter
The raven flies with the north star

See the Mark

A prayer for crying now
A tear on the rocking chair
The island is where the sound
Meets mountains, hills and valleys fair
Dances are danced
And songs are sung
Time will make me smile
Color me just for fun
To share a moment
To catch a star
The music box goes where pride takes it
Ride to the play on a street car

Sky the Star Catcher

It's dark
The stars are out
We got the night
So let's sing and shout
Gracie Bull
Madam ice
Lost is the vision
But only once or twice
Sweet is the dance
See how they skate
Ballet with sunshine
Grace is never late
So let's race for music
Dance for a song
Beauty in the body
With arms and legs so strong

Yes There Are Colors

What is orange
Maybe a pigeon flying across a carnival dress
Sun shining on mountains in the Wild West
Morning glow on an eagle's nest
Take me to a farmer's field
Where green rises under bare feet
Where nature and sunshine find a place to meet
Where we grow crops of barley and wheat
The owl's eyes are focused
Brown is the color of his wings
The owl is concentrating on only one thing
The prey and the meal it will bring
Colors grow bright and then they fade
Light and dark sun shine and shade
Colorful walls where bricks are laid
Look at the picture the little girl made

The Waves Crashing Down

Hemmingway is a pharaoh
In a book in an ancient evening
Music creeps into the room
This sound, this stage, is all in the seeing
We can find beauty
In the words of a slave
It's a story that must be told
The writer writes in words that are brave
It's a story of human respect
An element of desire
The light bulb goes off
With the poetry of a wood fire
What makes him so mellow
What makes him so good
The seagull flies over the sea
Quiet times in the neighborhood

Winter Fun

Engine against engine
A battle of gasoline might
Forced to take the plunge
Or make a rush toward a red light
Horses pull against oxen steady
Don't trust the driver to ask why
This the song that cries for peace
"Wind in the Pine" will never lie
So start the ball to roll
And fall in love with your water gun
We see it from the bottom of our soul
Round two of winter fun

The Minotaur

The Minotaur's eyes are wide
His teeth are sharp and full
He belongs in a mountain meadow
Hiding behind sheep's wool
The Minotaur's horns are wide
Ready to start a fight
The midnight move is heard
Against the glow of the moonlight
The Minotaur causes havoc
His hooves paw the ground
He threatens to charge and harm
The villagers in the quiet town

His First Step

He took his first step
Today to his daddies arms
He's funny, shy to himself
But believing in his charms
Go twenty years beyond
Whiskey and lace carry him down
A hopeless romantic enjoying life
Tying him softly to the ground
I shook my fist
A dominate arm smothered in style
It's a little easy to feel right
Easy to walk a mile

The Door Opens

Climb up on ugly mountain
To see the bear and the turtle dove
Wake me up in the dead of the night
Where a little white church has steeple right
In front of spirits above
Give our horse freedom
Harness to a carriage bright
Start at the bottom and work to the top
Find courage and never stop
Seeing the torch that carries the light
So read it forward
And read it again
Many words tell a story told
Times that circle down a country road
The love we give is love we send

The Page Remains Unread

We got up before the sun
Because we like the dark
Let's us do a brand new day
Say hello to a special mark
Go to a cup of coffee
Monday morning distress
It's a closely guarded secret
So act normal more or less
There's us
To take care of a wind that blew
Across troubled waters
A new freedom for me and you

The only Heaven I Know

The brownest eye
Sees a rebellion that's clear
Sees a world that's dear
Fights for togetherness that's very near
Universal change
Goes where it goes
Gives warmth to our toes
Gives meaning to a book of prose
So close the door behind me
And feel the warm breeze
Of the wind blowing through the trees
Truth and beauty the brownest eye sees

Thanks To You

Going through the motions
Fighting for emotional love
The cross on the steeple is high
Shining on all from above
Touched by your innocence
Something I can't lose
It's a promise from my heart
That sends us only good news
But everything is green
Under snow and barren trees
I close my eyes and dream
That I will taste honey from the honey bees

Revisit Your Wisdom

I saw my breath
Shadow beauty and truth
Of this town, this stage
Where stardom is the rage
Get your tickets from the ticket booth
What part do you want to sing
We heard the background noise
Sing the devil's sound
Make it come full circle around
Flashing light fights for the boys
Skipping rocks by the railroad track
See a love where you stay by me
Stand by stand the biggest star
Where it makes you what you are
Night on the town by the sparkling sea

Promise to Solve

I counted to one
Then came you
Walk with a stick in hand
With eyes the color blue
Clearly I see my mind
Directed by a higher power
Listening is an act of love
Hoping it will never grow sour
I can't go to Sunday school today
But I can sleep on a soft pillow
Hug me, I want to come back
To doze with the weeping willow
So no down time for you
Just a warm cup of tea
The story told is always true
Flying high with the honey bee

Survival Begins

The rain and the water
And leaves floating down
Ducks and ducklings
With hawks flying around
He deliberately turned away
The partner of the dance
Nature on line
Survival at a glance
Visit the winter
Come in from the cold
What if culture didn't mater
And ancient Vikings weren't so bold

Carry On in the World

Crystal ball on the table
Eyes that see clear
Walk a mile down a dirt road
Our memories are very near
Fill the words concisely
In truth and subtle ways
Figure eights and knots
Portend to happier days
Wave to the climber
Power of the dog
What seems like tomorrow
Is only time lost in the fog

We Weren't Looking

We should shine on
The book of make believe
Words that tell of long ago
Songs we sing when maidens weave
Does anybody hang out with God?
In a shelter where she writes
Night flying birds cross the sea
And fly against the city lights
Carefully build a fire
To fight darkness a blackboard away
I can't go back to that room in the sky
So make the ball roll
And live a sunny day

Die hard Drive

Act in a film
Rise and fall
In less than a flash
A message for us all
A sense of time
To our device
We tell the truth
Only once or twice
When divided into two
Who will take her place
The value of astonishment
Gone without a trace

My Special Friend

Let's hold hands
And change everything
Build a world
Where we laugh and sing
Unlock the mystery
And open the door
To a magic place
Where condors soar
Waves crash
Between the dark of the night
I wish everything would change
On the moon and starlight
Too tired to fight
Unwilling to cry
Happy to give
Love a try

Friends in a Flower Box

Daisies, pansies
Irises of blue
Tulips and marigolds
They live there too
Water them regularly
And dig the weeds
Our flowers grow tall
From tiny seeds
So altogether
They live as one
Friends in a box
Kissed by the sun

Tell My Story

The rope on the carpet
The foot goes there
Develop the step, the feeling is strong
The action encompasses a patchwork where
The hourglass is invisible
And time stands still
Tell him the truth again and again
They hold on to their story against their will
So welcome to paradise
The song plays true
Wake up this morning
To who we are and a joy that's new

Proud To Take A Stand

If you follow the stars
You'll be alright
It's what we dream of
Sailors delight
Did you think I would remember
Faith and a heavenly light
The best side of everything we do
Will open the doors to start light bright
Meet me in the middle
It would be cool if you did
I could listen to you all night long
And see where your memories are hid
Love is where the grass is green
A place where everything is real
Like a postcard out of nowhere
The warmth of the sun is what we feel

Live in Seasons Past

The warmth of the fire
A glow in the night
Watch the flames rise into the sky
Warm me in the fire light
Talk to me
Like lovers do
Make it sweet
With eyes of blue
Hear my voice
Say many things
Like hearing the sound
Of a humming birds wings
We see the monkey
With extraordinary eyes
He lives in the shadows
Where nature tells no lies

Finish What You Start

Can't you feel it
It's all around me
Can't you see it
It's everything we can be
Loyal friends of welcoming rooms
Shine on a guiding light
Open our thoughts to the outside
Find a diamond that is bright
There's a passion for what is possible
A need for an open mind
Shocked to see the heat of the chase
Look for a statue the ancient can find

A Hundred Years Ago

Flashback to Juliette
Love a hundred years ago
Dance to the troupadore
Taking it nice and slow
Devoted and loyal
Learn how to love
Swing to a past life
With the touch of a golden glove
The drive of hard rock music
Is not for you and me
But soft tunes and melodies
Will drift across an open sea

Winters Grip

Only the lonely
Know how I feel
Tap and blues
Heart of steel
Finding a way
To learn to love again
Boys will be boys
Love your fellow man
The storm carves out
The width of the stream
Moving water
Fisherman's dream
So talk to me
And hear my lonely song
I dream of grass that's green
And the grip of winter's long

Desperately in Need of Humbling

Black smoke rises higher and higher
Flames lick around the wall
We're at the eleventh hour
Time is here for us all
There's a good spirit here
Let us say what we think
Attitude is everything
The dance fan is the link
So many recordings
Of so many strings
All things invented
Melodies the young girl sings
I will not take sides
When song writers write a song
Pure poetry lives in the sun
Never let our world go wrong

Country Sun

Hang on to sunshine
For another day
Make it warm and cozy
With words only the lonely will say
Hot air balloons rise and fall
Their colors grace the sky
We watch them float in the wind
The adventure is ours, see them fly
Nancy my sweet is writing a book
Pages of dreams that are coming true
Dottie and Rubbie live in the sun
Angels and fairies live there too
So put the good
In all this crazy stuff
The love you give
Is always enough

Wooden Boats

You don't have to cry
In a mystical world that wonders why
Forced to look at moving pain
Art in our vision is our gain
Join us on the battlefield
Fighting for the spinning wheel
Special moment, special friend
Competing for love to the end
The way she writes the paperback book
Pages turn so let's take a look
So things are bending, bowing, and breaking
A turn towards justice in the making
But no amount of gold that we steel
Will equal the passion that we feel

Between Me and My Work

Just not now
The target said in her magic moment
She said "Bring your old golden ball"
A looseness of desire, a fall in decent
What has he done
He has given them so much
Next morning her eyes will open wide
To a powerful force and a soft touch
Speak out, the adventure awaits
The high flier keeps her strong
We can still see you, glass child
See you breeze down a road that's long

Robert's Idea

The brave warrior came by
And knocked on my door
Red Cloud the chief
Of western nations and Indian loor
The banjo player strummed
An universal tune
A quiet sound we all can hear
Together under a harvest moon
Someday it will all be good
Sailing along in ships of blue
Anytime now the lights will be bright
This poet dreams for me and you

Sounds of Spring

Let me hide behind sunken eyes
Rock of ages, clear and dry
The beauty of yesterday and today
Tells us tales of wondering why
Soft flowers in a day in June
Inspiring sounds of the bumble bee
We can't get away from singing
Songs that say "We all can be free"
Orange morning start the day
The sunlight sees birds in flight
Spring day comes into view
See the flight of the paper kite

City Limits

God is a grey beard in the clouds
A warhorse in the sky
Who will save them now
The city of a million will tell us why
Some day we'll build a castle
With walls and an iron door
Jack Johnson is never a hassle
My poems, his songs for ever more
Something new
Will break something old
The color blue
Shines on a song of silver and gold

Two Birds on a Limb

I drew a picture
Trying to be the best
Colors flew off the page
I looked to the west
Two birds on a limb
Flowers with them too
Dear Nancy our sweet
The birds in a sky of blue
Take a walk down a path
Bare feet in the chill
The water looks cold
Wild animals test our will
Joy comes, grief goes
Everybody is happy now
To be thankful for grass to be green
And the gratitude that love will allow

Where Do You Turn

I saw James' rough red cheek
In sleep's so beautiful and fair
Trusty and trustworthy in front of my mind
Your eyes are unique, quietly we stare
The problem has no name
The solution can never be
Larger and larger is our power
To sail a boat across the sea
The time was right
People will rise up and sing
Stand up and make some noise
Singing is a wonderful thing

One Dream Away

Love is fragile
Like a dandelion in a breeze
One taper lights a thousand stars
The adventure lives in a forest of trees
See the good
The beauty is surreal
Come see how pretty we are
See the spin of a bicycle wheel
I'm your best day ever
Stormy skies, make them go away
See your all time high prevail
Walk down a path to a sunny day

Other Whispers

The northern violet shall blow
Above his humble grave
Ah, the thrust of a fickle love
See once more with a blossoming wave
To draw upon a moment's pause
And the walk of five hundred miles aside
Writers draw a sudden change
When sailing through this stormy ride
The lady felt a rattle in the window
And the dance of the waltz of spring
Simple solders full of color
It's fun to do this wonderful thing

The Wind and a Fallen Tree

The crooked footpath turns
To the wind and a fallen tree
Rocks across the pathway lie
In front of the steps that we see
And yet there were no answers heard
A word or an errant line
The empty life, the shallow plane
His power is the dream we find
Does heaven seem blind and dumb?
Does God not show the way?
But the factor will triumph and prevail
Praying for peace, hear the words we say

All the Things I Want to Write

I dragged a comb across my head
Then let the fiddle come alive
Taste the alphabet soup
And take the horse on a drive
I will see what my sweetheart will do
When dance and jive will play to a song
Write a tale that never ends
And paint a picture in colors very strong
Spring will come behind the snow
Flowers from dirt will bloom in the sun
Water will cleanse the soul of fire
And love will find a voice and be the one

Spin the Wheel

Wild wears the dress
Of a ghost letter
I'm proud to play a song
So glad to see us live together
Give me a day pass to heaven
I want to see the stars converge
Take a voyage to Mars today
Our lens sees the rocket ship surge
Give me your book
A ninety minute slam
Something good, something real
The woodcutter lives with the lamb

A Cup of Joy

The things we say
The things we do
It's a lesson in life
For me and you
Feel the breeze
Blow through the night
Down a road that's long
A vision of starlight
Back when the game was played
And the winners were strong
A hundred days have passed
And the best were never wrong
So enjoy the things
We say and do
The love we remember
Will always be true

Kisses are Blue

We were once young
But now we're old
Watching your all time high
Is the story told
The craziest thing I ever did
Was writing love letters in your book
I'm part of what the young man says
Birds in the sky, so let's take a look
Every day the sun shines again
But heaven is still so far
Wishing that all things will pass
And that we're all as bright as a star
It started with a good night kiss
So let's spend all night
Dreaming of things that I will remember
Things like sun, sand and moonlight

Before the Age of Caring

Swifter than light
In a timeless way
Waiting with wings and watchful eyes
Free is the message we give everyday
Two sets of rules
Find a voice
Too mean or mighty
Is always the choice
The truest steps are human
We reach in the child's sky
Louder, faster, slower, warmer
Up and down the hill we fly
As God is true
Hope will come
The gate keeper rules
Under an iron thumb

Book Your Trip

In life's early morn
Is the night of the dark
Every piece of what we do
Is a footstep closer to the mark
Standing on the corner, crying
Going one time, flying
I cannot say, I will not say
That art is long
And seeing it is the way
Every back road in this town
Leads to Yokum Lake
Swing on by the waters edge
Passionately is the love we make

Six Months and a Grave

Step close to the easy chair
For the future opens fair and wide
Rock of ages, feel the words
Extravagance finds nowhere to hide
With quivering breath
And a sobering brow
A lovely animal
For the here and now
There comes a glad whisper
Being more is relevant today
Create a world around the brave
Six months and a grave shows us the way

Cling to a System

Thunder falls on castle walls
The rain loosens the strong
Sweet makes us step up close
To a snowy summit high and long
Her voice seemed dark
Low and weak with a haunting sound
Her emotional joy is lost in life
A turbulent sunset shines on the town
Quick was the fall
From peace and the comfort zone
The camera shows a vision
The image of black stone

Little More Action

She gave me a cup of kindness
A tap of her finger and so much more
I was waiting for someone to feel
The chill wind from a far off shore
Sunlit fades on a dirt road
Shadows grow against a wall
Worked all week to play
Games that made winners of us all
Sweetness is hers
With good stuff, song, and a good time
The fairest flower will bloom bright
And hear the song of the wind chime

Its just for sleep

Rock me to sleep
With songs of many knocks
Smile in the summer months
Where doors have many locks
Blossomed and faded is our face between
The circles around the light
Wisdom and counsel will always live
Quietly along a starlit night
Pierced in the heart
With words stronger than steel
A war of mankind
Is fought with a spinners wheel